iMath
Readers

S0-CFK-476

On the Playground:
How Do You Build Place Value?

by Donna Loughran

Content Consultant
David T. Hughes
Mathematics Curriculum Specialist

NORWOOD HOUSE PRESS
Chicago, IL

Norwood House Press
PO Box 316598
Chicago, IL 60631

For information regarding Norwood House Press, please visit our website at
www.norwoodhousepress.com or call 866-565-2900.

Special thanks to: Heidi Doyle
Production Management: Six Red Marbles
Editors: Linda Bullock and Kendra Muntz
Printed in North Mankato, Minnesota. 295R—062016

Paperback ISBN: 978-1-60357-488-4

The Library of Congress has cataloged the original hardcover edition with the following
call number: 2012023837

CONTENTS

Note to Caregivers:

Throughout this book, many questions are posed to the reader. Some are open-ended and ask what the reader thinks. Discuss these questions with your child and guide him or her in thinking through the possible answers and outcomes. There are also questions posed which have a specific answer. Encourage your child to read through the text to determine the correct answer. Most importantly, encourage answers grounded in reality while also allowing imaginations to soar. Information to help support you as you share the book with your child is provided in the back in the **Additional Notes** section.

Bold words are defined in the glossary in the back of the book.

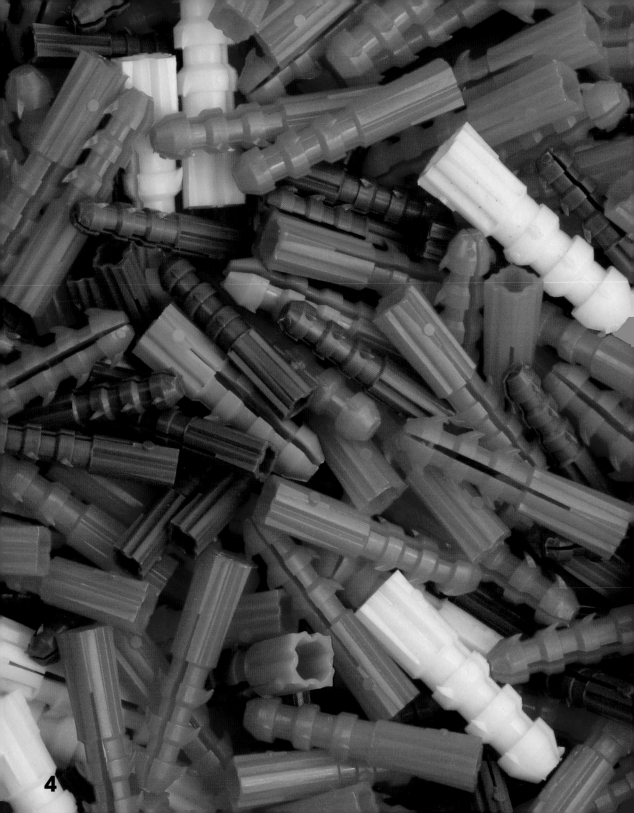

A New Playground Set

Mr. Bryan is a builder. He is also Henry and Sasha's dad.

Mr. Bryan is building a new playground for Henry and Sasha's school. But Mr. Bryan needs their help. He wants to finish the playground before school starts. He has measurements to make. He has problems to solve. And he has things to put together.

Mr. Bryan uses lots of numbers in his work. A number has **digits**. There are ten digits in all:

0, 1, 2, 3, 4, 5, 6, 7, 8, 9

In a number, each digit has a **place value**. The place value tells you how much the digit stands for.

In this book, you will learn about place value. Understanding place value will help you understand numbers in different ways.

Counting Hundreds, Tens, and Ones

Mr. Bryan needs many, many plugs. He will use them to join the pieces of the playground together.

Mr. Bryan tells Henry and Sasha that he needs 212 yellow plugs to build the slide. How will they gather that many plugs?

Screws come in different sizes. Screws fit into plugs. Each size plug has a different color.

Idea 1: Henry and Sasha can use **place-value blocks**.

They collect 2 hundred blocks, 1 ten block, and 2 ones.

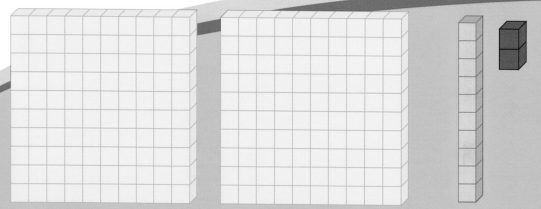

Do you think this is a good way to model 212? Why or why not?

Idea 2: Henry and Sasha can use **beansticks** to show place value.

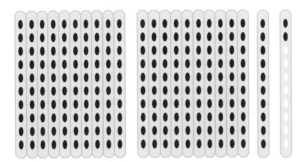

Do you think this is a good way to model 212? Why or why not?

Idea 3: Henry and Sasha can use **linking cubes** to show place value.

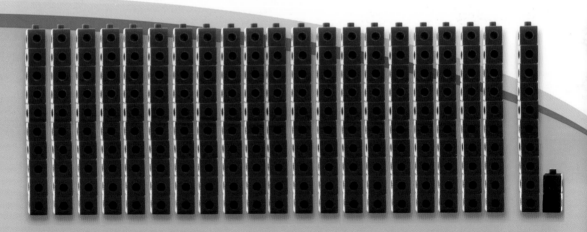

Do you think this is a good way to model 212? Why or why not?

Discover Activity

Materials
- pencil
- paper
- three number cubes

Roll Place Values

Play a game with a friend or family member. Take turns.

Roll three number cubes. Put them side by side. Write and say the number they make.

Let's use the number cubes in the picture as an example. You can put the cubes side by side to make the number 321. You would say the words "three hundred twenty-one." Give yourself one point if you say the number correctly.

Now, tell how many hundreds, tens, and ones are in 321. There are 3 hundreds, 2 tens, and 1 one. Give yourself an extra point if you are correct.

Now let your friend take a turn.

The first player to earn 15 points is the winner.

Building Place Value

Mr. Bryan says, "Henry and Sasha, I need red plugs now. Will you bring me 54 red plugs, please?"

How many groups of ten are there in 54? How many ones are there? Use place-value blocks to find the answer.

Tens	Ones

Tens	Ones
5	4

Next, Mr. Bryan says, "Henry and Sasha, I need more plugs. I have three red roofs to put together. I need 330 red plugs in all."

How many hundreds are in the number 330? How many tens? How many ones? Use beansticks to find the answer.

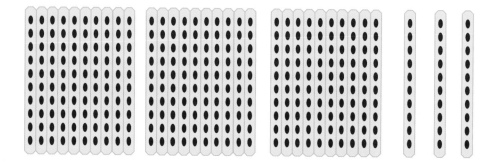

 Did You Know?

Some children play marble games on playgrounds. People have played with marbles for 3,000 years!

Greater Than and Less Than

Mr. Bryan added a giant box in his playground plans. He plans to fill the box with colorful balls. There will be 61 green balls and 58 blue balls. There will be red and yellow balls, too.

You can use place value to compare numbers. Place value tells you if a number is **greater than** (>) or **less than** (<), or equal to (=) another number.

There will be 61 green balls. There will be 58 blue balls.

Compare the tens. Which number is greater, 6 tens or 5 tens? Use linking cubes to show the numbers 61 and 58.

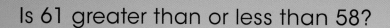

Is 61 greater than or less than 58?

Say they added 150 red balls and 130 yellow balls. Which number is greater? Compare the hundreds first. They are the same. Each number has one group of 100. Compare the tens next. Which is greater, 5 tens or 3 tens? Is 150 greater than or less than 130?

Math at Work

There are many different kinds of playgrounds. All playgrounds start as an idea. Builders sketch their ideas on paper. Then, they make special drawings. These drawings are called **blueprints**. You can think of a blueprint as a building plan.

Mr. Bryan, for example, didn't start building right away. Instead, he made a blueprint. He measured carefully to know how much space there was for the playground. Then, he planned what would fit in the space.

He measured other things, too. Wood. Rope. Plastic pipes. Boards. Every measurement was exact. Why do you think Mr. Bryan measured so carefully before he began building?

Connecting to History

Have you ever had a ride on a **carousel** [KAA-ruh-sell]? A carousel is a kind of merry-go-round. People ride painted wooden animals. Music plays as the animals go round and round.

The oldest carousel in the United States is in Rhode Island. It is called the Flying Horse Carousel. It was made in 1876.

The Flying Horse Carousel has 20 horses in all. They do not move up and down on poles. Instead, they hang from a frame at the center of the carousel. When the carousel spins, the horses fly.

Each horse is carved from wood. Its mane and tail are made of real horsehair. Its saddle is made of leather. And its eyes are made of stones.

Would you like to ride on a carousel like this?

Some modern carousels still have wooden animals like these horses.

What's the Word?

It is always fun to swing on a playground.

Robert Louis Stevenson must have liked to swing, too.
He wrote this poem.

The Swing

How do you like to go up in a swing

Up in the air so blue?

Oh, I do think it the pleasantest thing

Ever a child can do!

Up in the air and over the wall,

Till I can see so wide,

River and trees and cattle and all

Over the countryside–

Till I look down on the garden green

Down on the roof so brown–

Up in the air I go flying again,

Up in the air and down!

Do you enjoy going up in a swing as much as this boy does?

Playground Fun

Sasha, Henry, and their friends like to play hopscotch. So, Mr. Bryan painted a hopscotch board for them.

In all, 102 children played hopscotch in one week. The next week, 104 children played. Which number is less, 102 or 104?

Basketball is fun to play on the playground, too. Henry and his friends shoot baskets. They give themselves one point for every ball that goes through the net.

In one game, Henry got 22 points. Tanisha got 19 points. Martin got 21 points.

Of those three players, who got the most points?

Can you put these scores in order from least to greatest? 22, 19, 21

These children play basketball on a playground. What games do you like to play on the playground?

iMath Ideas: Count Them All

Mr. Bryan finished the yellow slides. He put together the red roofs. Then, it was time to work on the ladders.

"Henry and Sasha," he called. "Will you please bring me 384 gray plugs?"

The children's eyes opened wide. Mr. Bryan saw the children looking at him. He chuckled. "You can count 384 plugs," he said. "Think about the different ways you can do it."

Idea 1: "You can use **place-value blocks**," said Mr. Bryan. "How many hundreds blocks will you need? How many tens blocks? How many ones? Then, you can find matching numbers of plugs."

Place-value blocks make counting easy and fast. Henry and Sasha can use place-value blocks to figure out how many plugs their dad needs.

Idea 2: "Or, you can use **beansticks** to figure out how many plugs to get," Mr. Bryan said.

"Dad is right," Sasha said. "But that's a lot of beans! And it will take a long time!"

Idea 3: "Or you can use **linking cubes** to show how many plugs to get," Mr. Bryan added.

"Dad is right again," said Henry. "But I don't want to snap many cubes together."

"Then, we'll use **place-value blocks**!" Sasha said.

How many hundreds, tens, and ones are in 384?

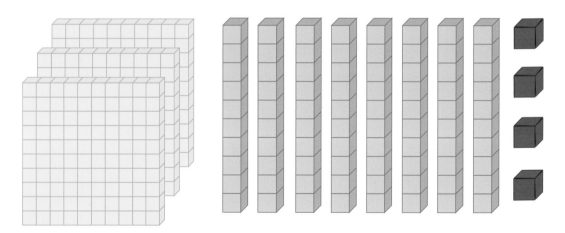

At last, the playground is finished. Mr. Bryan did a great job. So did Henry and Sasha. Now it's time to play!

What Comes Next?

Imagine building new objects for a playground. Make a plan. Begin with questions.

1. What would the object do?

2. How would children use it?

3. How could you make it so that all children could use it?

4. How many children could use it at one time?

5. How could you make it safe for all children?

6. What kinds of building materials would you need?

Draw a picture of the object. Describe what it is made of. Use cardboard to make a model.

Visit a building store with an adult. Or search the Internet together. Find out if you could build the object you designed. You could make your own playground fun!

GLOSSARY

beansticks: wooden counting tools that can hold up to 10 beans.

blueprints: plans that builders follow to build things like houses and parks.

carousel: a merry-go-round with carved animals that people can ride.

digits: symbols we use when we write numbers. There are ten digits: 0, 1, 2, 3, 4, 5, 6, 7, 8, 9.

greater than: more than. For example, 4 is greater than 3.

less than: fewer than. For example, 5 is less than 9.

linking cubes: cubes that snap together. You can use them to show place value.

place value: the value of a digit in a number. For example, the digit 3 in 135 stands for 3 tens. It has a value of 30.

place-value blocks: blocks that show hundreds, tens, and ones.

FURTHER READING

Fiction

Builder Goose: It's Construction Rhyme Time!, by Boni Ashburn, Sterling Children's Books, 2012

Playground Day, by Jennifer Merz, Houghton Mifflin Harcourt, 2007

Nonfiction

Job Site, by Nathan Clement, Boyds Mills Press, 2011

Place Value: The Next Stage, by Claire Piddock, Crabtree Publishing Company, 2010

Additional Notes

The page references below provide answers to questions asked throughout the book. Questions whose answers will vary are not addressed.

Page 9: There are 5 groups of ten and 4 ones in 54.

Page 10: There are 3 hundreds, 3 tens, and 0 ones.

Page 12: 61 is greater than 58. Five tens is greater than 3 tens. 150 is greater than 130.

Page 17: 102 is less than 104.

Page 18: Henry got the most points. From least to greatest, the numbers are 19, 21, 22.

Page 20: There are 3 hundreds, 8 tens, and 4 ones in 384.

INDEX

Content Consultant

David T. Hughes

David is an experienced mathematics teacher, writer, presenter, and adviser. He serves as a consultant for the Partnership for Assessment of Readiness for College and Careers. David has also worked as the Senior Program Coordinator for the Charles A. Dana Center at The University of Texas at Austin and was an editor and contributor for the *Mathematics Standards in the Classroom* series.